From the movie

Disney

FROZEN

MEGA
Colouring

PaRragon

Bath · New York · Cologne · Melbourne · Delhi
Hong Kong · Shenzhen · Singapore · Amsterdam

Elsa and Anna are sisters. They love playing together.

Elsa has magical powers – she can freeze things
and make snow!

Elsa uses her magic to build a snowman for her sister.
His name is Olaf.

While they're playing, Elsa accidentally hits Anna with an icy blast.

Their parents, the king and queen of Arendelle, rush the girls to see the trolls. Their magic can help Anna.

The trolls help Anna and they change her memories so she'll forget about Elsa's magic. Elsa must wear gloves to block her powers.

The king closes the castle doors and builds walls
around Arendelle. The girls aren't allowed to leave.

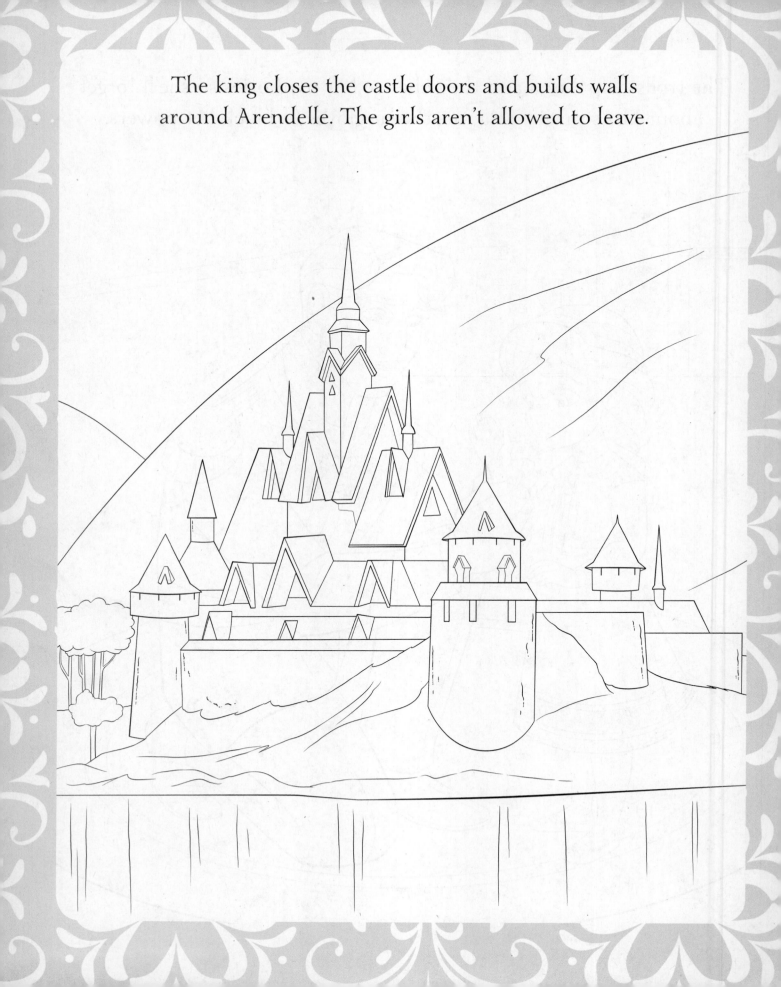

Elsa is scared she will hurt her sister again,
so she decides not to play with Anna any more.

Anna asks Elsa again and again if they can play together,
but Elsa is too scared. As they get older, the sisters grow apart.

After their parents are lost at sea, Elsa is to be crowned queen.
She worries she won't be able to hide her powers at the coronation.

Princess Anna is dressed up for her sister's coronation.

Anna is thrilled that the castle gates are open for the occasion.
She can't wait to explore and meet new people.

Prince Hans has sailed to Arendelle from afar for the celebrations.

Princess Anna runs into Hans's horse and falls into a boat,
but Hans is very pleased to meet her.

Anna rushes back to the castle and arrives just in time for the coronation – she makes quite an entrance!

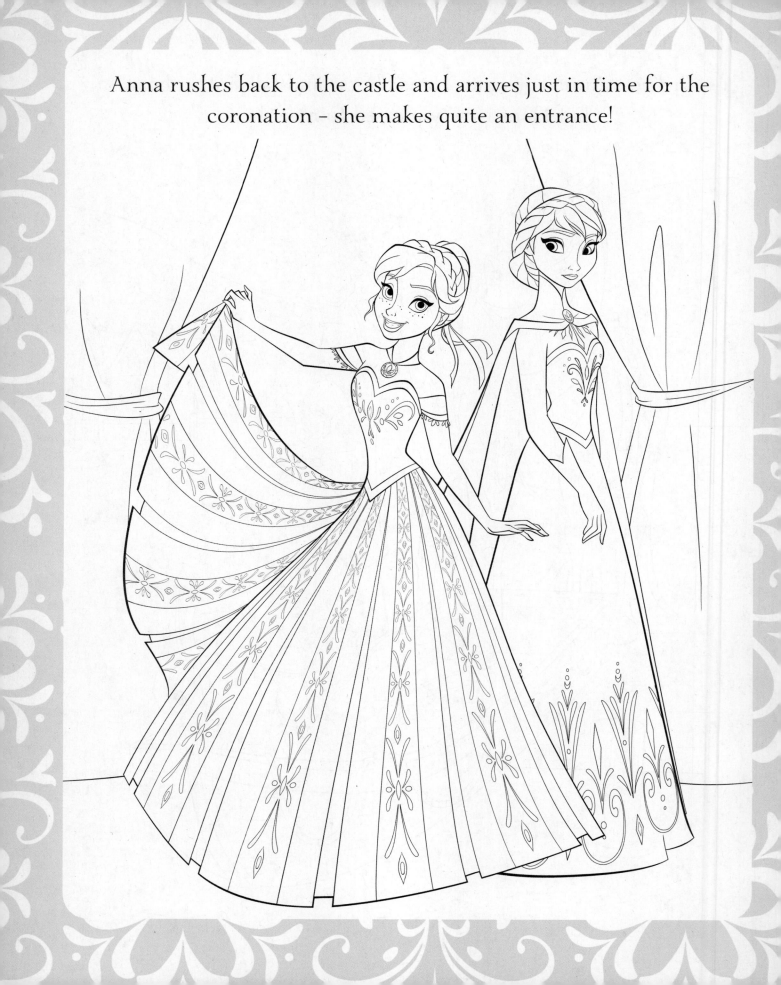

Elsa holds the sceptre and orb in her bare hands without freezing them, while Anna stands by her side.

Elsa is proud to be queen of Arendelle and relieved that she has managed to hide her powers.

Princess Anna and Prince Hans share a dance at the coronation celebrations. Anna is sure this is true love.

Later, after a long walk, Hans asks
Anna to marry him. She says yes!

Anna tells Elsa that she and Prince Hans are engaged.
But Elsa does not approve.

As the sisters argue, Anna pulls off one of Elsa's gloves.

When Anna asks her sister what she's so afraid of, Elsa loses
control and accidentally blasts ice everywhere.

The people of Arendelle are frightened of Elsa's powers.
Even Anna is shocked to finally learn her sister's secret.

Queen Elsa runs away from Arendelle. She is scared people will hurt her – and that she could hurt them. As she leaves, snow and ice cover the ground behind her.

Anna decides she must go after her sister. She asks Hans to take care of the kingdom while she is away.

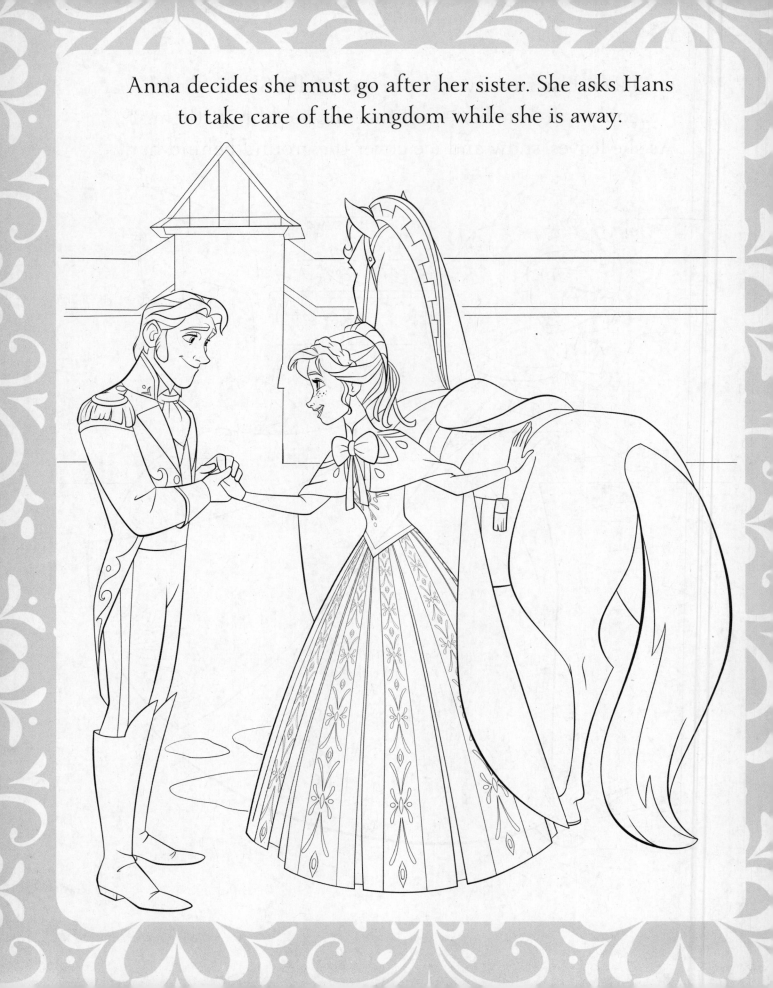

The further Elsa runs from Arendelle, the freer she feels.
She doesn't have to hide any more.

Elsa can finally use her powers properly.
She builds a stunning ice palace on the North Mountain.

Then Elsa transforms her hair and her dress.
She becomes the Snow Queen!

Meanwhile, Princess Anna battles through
the icy storm in the mountains.

Anna is thrown from her horse and lands in the snow.
Luckily, she finds shelter in a remote shop.

Oaken is the owner of the shop, which sells supplies to travellers.
He is a jolly man - just don't make him mad.

Anna meets a snow-covered Kristoff inside the shop.
He knows where the storm is coming from.

Kristoff is an expert mountain man, as well as an ice harvester. He is not happy about the storm – it's very bad for business.

Kristoff's best friend is a reindeer called Sven. Sven loves carrots!

Kristoff calls Oaken a 'crook' and is thrown out of the shop.

Anna thinks Kristoff will be able to help her find Elsa.
She asks for his help and gives Sven some carrots to persuade them.

Kristoff agrees to help Anna and they set off in his sledge.

On the journey, they find they have a lot to talk about.

But their conversation is interrupted when
a pack of wolves starts chasing them!

The wolf chase ends with a terrible crash.
Anna and Sven pull Kristoff to safety.

Kristoff loses his sledge and most of his possessions. Anna promises to replace everything and Kristoff agrees to keep helping her.

Meanwhile, Anna's horse returns to Arendelle without her.

Hans gathers a group of men and they set off to find Princess Anna.

Back on the mountain, the three new friends find Elsa's icy wonderland – and a walking, talking snowman called Olaf!

Olaf is a magical snowman who likes warm hugs.

Olaf may be made of snow, but he'd love to
spend time relaxing in the summer sun.

Sven and Olaf quickly become friends –
even though Sven tries to eat Olaf's carrot nose!

Anna notices that Olaf looks just like the snowman Elsa made for her when they were children. She realizes that her new friend has been created by her sister!

Olaf shows Anna, Kristoff and Sven the way to the ice palace. Anna is determined to find Elsa.

The ice palace looks magnificent at the top of the North Mountain.
Anna can't believe what her sister has created.

Anna, Kristoff, Sven and Olaf meet Elsa the Snow Queen.

Anna asks Elsa to return to Arendelle but Elsa refuses.
She thinks it is too dangerous for everyone.

Anna won't give up. She wants her sister to come home
so they can be friends and so Elsa can stop the winter!

Elsa knows she can never be close to Anna.
She grows more and more angry and accidentally
fires an icy blast that hits Anna in the heart.

Even though she is hurt, Anna refuses to leave.
She's still worried about Elsa.

Elsa builds a giant snowman called Marshmallow to escort them from the palace. Olaf thinks they can be friends!

Anna angers Marshmallow so he chases Anna and Kristoff away.

As they try to escape, Kristoff helps
Anna down the side of the mountain.

Elsa is upset about striking her sister with ice
and not being able to control her magic.

Anna, Kristoff, Sven and Olaf make it down safely.
Suddenly, Anna's hair starts to turn white.
Elsa's blast of ice has put a powerful curse on her.

Kristoff takes Anna to see his friends,
the trolls. They are magical healers.

The oldest troll is the one who can help
Anna the most. He has seen this magic before.

The old troll is worried. He says Anna will soon freeze completely!
Only an act of true love will thaw a frozen heart.

Anna starts to freeze from within. Kristoff rushes her back to Arendelle. A true love's kiss from Hans should save her.

Meanwhile, the royal guards have arrived at the ice palace.
Elsa sends Marshmallow to greet them.

Some of the guards get past Marshmallow and threaten Elsa.

Elsa uses her powers to defend herself. She pins one of the guards against the wall with icy blades. Hans stops her from hurting him.

Hans asks Elsa to return home and stop the
winter freeze. But Elsa doesn't want to go back.

One of the guards fires an arrow at Elsa, but instead it hits a chandelier that falls on top of the Snow Queen.

Hans takes Elsa back to Arendelle. He locks her in
a dungeon to protect the kingdom from her magic.

Kristoff takes Anna to the castle gates, where the royal staff take her inside. The two friends find it hard to say goodbye.

Anna explains everything to Hans
and asks him to kiss her. He refuses!

Hans reveals his evil plan. He never really loved Anna –
he only wanted to take over the kingdom. He puts out
the fire so Anna will freeze faster.

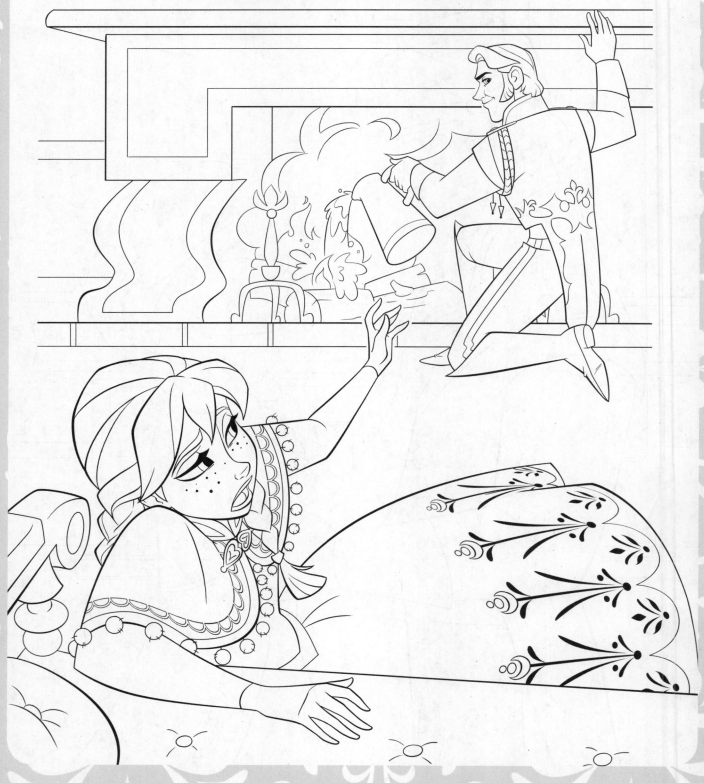

Hans leaves and locks the door. Anna wants to warn Elsa, but she doesn't have the strength. She's getting colder every second.

Elsa decides she is too dangerous to stay in Arendelle.
She uses her magic to blast out of the dungeon.

Halfway up the mountain, Sven tries to convince Kristoff to return to Arendelle. The reindeer knows that Kristoff loves Anna.

Back in the castle, Olaf has arrived to help Anna. He looks out of the window and sees Sven and Kristoff running back towards Arendelle. Kristoff must love Anna!

Anna realizes that she loves Kristoff, too! Olaf helps her climb out of the window. Kissing Kristoff is Anna's only hope.

Anna is freezing fast! Can an act of true love really save her?

Hans finds Elsa as she is running away.
He tells Elsa her blast of ice has killed Anna.

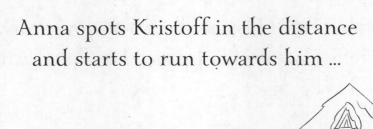

Anna spots Kristoff in the distance
and starts to run towards him ...

... but Anna sees that Elsa is in danger as Hans sneaks up behind her. Anna must help her sister, but without Kristoff's kiss, she will die.

Hans raises his sword, preparing to strike Elsa.

Anna runs over to save Elsa and jumps in front
of Hans's sword, just as she freezes solid.

Elsa hugs her frozen sister and cries as she realizes
that Anna has saved her life. But then, Anna starts to thaw.

Anna's act of true love in saving her sister
has broken the spell. Anna is no longer frozen!

Hans is the one with the frozen heart and
Anna never wants to see him again.

Anna has taught Elsa about love and not being afraid.
Elsa can now control her magic, so she brings back summer.

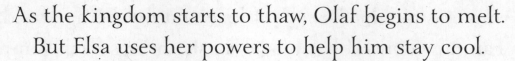

As the kingdom starts to thaw, Olaf begins to melt.
But Elsa uses her powers to help him stay cool.

Kristoff, Anna, Elsa and even Olaf are happy
that summer has returned to Arendelle.

Anna keeps her promise and gives Kristoff a new sledge.
He decides to stay in Arendelle – with Anna!

Anna thanks Sven for all his help, too, by giving him treats!

Finally, Anna and Elsa can play together again. Elsa creates a winter wonderland – just like she did when they were children.

They build a snowman – putting their friend Olaf
back together after a small accident!

Anna and Elsa are sisters – and friends. They'll never be apart again.